PODCAST ADVERTISING WORKS

How to Turn Engaged Audiences Into Loyal Customers

by

GLENN RUBENSTEIN

TABLE OF CONTENTS

BONUS OFFER

As a "thank you" for checking out my book, I'd like to give you the Executive Summary and an eBook version for FREE.

Please visit http://adopter.media/bookbonus to take advantage of this offer.

DEDICATION

To Lisa, for saying "hell yeah." Thank you for everything.

I also want to thank the following people, who this book would not have been possible without: Leo, Debi, Carly, and Frederique. Tiffany, Debby, and Danielle. Ray and Aaron. Tim and Don. Samantha, David, Lauren, and Julie. Mark and Mike. Jeffrey and Josh. Liz and Ryan. Marine and Rhett. Adam, Giovanni, Lex, Eli, Jeff, Scott, John, Jo Ann, Robert, Ken, Mark, Adam, and Chantel.

And thank you for reading this book and your interest in podcast advertising.

INTRODUCTION

The first podcast advertisement I heard was on *The Adam Carolla Show*. This was back in 2010.

The phrasing and introduction now seem so common, but I can remember when I first heard Adam say he wanted to take a moment and thank his sponsor.

It got my attention. *Who sponsors a podcast? People advertise on podcasts now?* I thought.

Up until that point, Adam Carolla's daily podcast seemed like it was just Adam having loose conversations and conducting interviews. It felt like hanging out with friends—so much so that his podcast was a part of my routine.

That first podcast ad I heard was for the ManGrate grill accessory. Adam told a story about a guy removing a grill from an old steakhouse and noticing the cast iron grill grates. He was curious what they were, so he did some research and realized that cooking on those grill grates is a big part of that "steakhouse" taste. He looked into manufacturing a version that would work for any home grill or BBQ, and the ManGrate was born.

Adam continued the spot, talking about how he had personally been using the ManGrate. He talked about how he tasted the difference, and everyone he knew who tried it agreed it was the superior way to grill. And of course, because the guys at

ManGrate were big fans of *The Adam Carolla Show*, they had a special deal for his audience.

After I heard this, I brought up the ManGrate to my friends and family. In casual conversation, I offered up that piece of trivia about the cast iron grates that steakhouses use. To anyone who showed even half interest, I mentioned the website and the offer for Adam Carolla fans. I hadn't just discovered something new, I felt like I had learned something.

Podcast advertising had an incredible effect on me from the first day I experienced it (and I didn't even work in podcasting at the time).

As far as the ManGrate grill-enhancement system was concerned, however, there was only one thing keeping me from ordering one for myself: I'm vegan.

But the vast majority of Adam Carolla fans are not, and ManGrate has since had a long history of sponsoring *The Adam Carolla Show*. Nothing speaks to success in advertising like repeat business, which tells me that ManGrate's ongoing sponsorship efforts with Adam's podcast have worked just as well—probably better—with the rest of his audience.

I started working in podcast advertising in 2012. Years later, I still think of this first podcast ad whenever I work with a new advertiser.

WHY I WROTE THIS BOOK

"You should write a book."

You hear that enough, and you start to believe you should.

This book represents the answers to questions I've gathered from hundreds of in-person meetings, thousands of phone calls, and tens of thousands of emails.

I started selling podcast advertising in 2012. I was working at TWiT as the Director of Marketing, and an opportunity arose to be a part of the CEO's recently formed in-house sales effort.

Within days, I had my first sales call. At the time, everything I knew about podcast advertising was from the ads that I had heard.

The first potential advertiser I spoke to had questions: How are podcast advertising rates determined? What shows should I be considering? How will I know if my ads are effective?

I sought out the answers.

The next potential advertiser had similar questions, plus a few more about the ad formats and audience.

By my third call with a potential advertiser, I had a stockpile of information, and I was able to educate them to the point of feeling confident moving forward with sponsoring a podcast. (To this day, they're still podcast advertisers.)

Part of the reason I wrote this book is my approach to ad sales. I don't like the term "salesman" or the perception that to sell is simply to persuade.

I prefer to educate people and build information-based relationships. I'm offering potential clients value, whether they choose to buy or not. When working with a client, I'm not out to simply make a sale; I'm looking to find and create opportunities where we can build success.

And that's what I do. It's not about facilitating the purchase of ads on a podcast. That's only one element of building success in this medium. I serve my clients every step of the way to help ensure the best results possible.

Dozens of advertisers, hundreds of campaigns, and millions of dollars in ad sales later, I'd say that my approach has worked.

In 2014, I started visiting advertisers and agencies for lunch-and-learn sessions. Since then, that's expanded to consulting with advertisers and traditional media agencies to educate them and help guide their podcast advertising plans, as well as starting ADOPTER Media, a full service podcast advertising agency.

I've heard countless times that there should be a book on podcast advertising and a few dozen people whose opinions I trust suggested that I write it.

Since no one is clamoring for "The Ultimate Vegan Guide to Steakhouse Grilling," I decided it was time to document the years of knowledge I've gained in podcast advertising.

This book will give you a complete overview of the terminology, styles, and best practices for podcast advertising. More importantly, it will outline how podcast advertising can convert engaged audiences into your loyal customers.

BACKGROUND

I spend hours each day educating people about podcast advertising. I'm not complaining, because I enjoy it.

I frequently speak with advertisers who don't know much about podcasts. On the flip side, I also speak with CEOs and marketers who are familiar with podcasts, but don't know much about traditional advertising.

If you work in marketing or advertising, the following chapters will quickly give you a comprehensive background on podcasting and podcast advertising.

If you're familiar with podcasts, you'll learn about how podcast advertising fits into the bigger picture of advertising across different forms of media.

A BRIEF HISTORY OF PODCASTING

Digital audio existed for decades before the MP3, but for our purposes, let's start in the mid-1990s. That's when MP3s became popular, largely due to music piracy.

In addition to music, talk radio fans shared unauthorized recordings of popular radio shows, including *The Howard Stern Show*, Art Bell's *Coast to Coast*, and *Loveline* with Adam Carolla and Dr. Drew.

At the same time, there was a streaming audio player named RealAudio that allowed anyone to stream live or on-demand audio through a dial-up internet connection. Many people were empowered to start internet radio stations, but there was a significant cost to purchase RealAudio's encoding software and set up a website to do the streaming.

In 1998, Nullsoft released a free MP3 streaming plugin named Shoutcast for its popular WinAmp MP3 software. With that, anyone with a computer and an internet connection could live stream high-quality music and talk via a personal online radio station.

It wasn't long before budding broadcasters started to stream and record online radio shows via Shoutcast and also make them available as MP3s for download. A small handful of lecturers, comedians, and storytellers started to do the same.

1998 was also the year that standalone MP3 players hit the market. That meant people no longer needed a computer for playback, and we could take our MP3s with us.

In the years that followed, MP3 players grew in popularity. Apple's iPod became a massive success, and bands and record labels started to release official MP3s for purchase, offering a much-needed alternative to piracy. (Yay, iTunes!) Some forward-thinking talk radio shows and stations also started to offer official MP3 recordings of their shows for download.

In 2004, original spoken-word MP3 content really took off.

The term **podcasting** was first mentioned by Ben Hammersley of **The Guardian** in a February 2004 article. It is a portmanteau (or mash-up) of the words **pod** from iPod and **cast** from broadcast.

Adam Curry's **Daily Source Code** podcast started in 2004. Leo Laporte's **This Week in Tech** released its first episode in 2005. iTunes began listing and offering podcasts in June of that year, and **podcast** was even named the New Oxford American Dictionary's Word of the Year.

For the most part, podcasting was still very niche. Remember, you either had to listen to a podcast on a computer, or you had to download the podcast to your computer and then transfer it via cable to your standalone MP3 player. (During this era, workouts and road trips suffered substantial delays due to prehistoric data transfer speeds.)

Many podcasts you've never heard of started and stopped. Companies launched and folded. By 2006, not many people were talking about podcasts anymore. YouTube had changed the conversation, and original internet video became the medium of the future.

In June 2007, the world changed. Apple introduced the iPhone, which allowed direct downloads and the ability to stream right to your device.

Whether it was music or talk, a world of audio possibilities was now instantly available.

In 2009, Adam Carolla's terrestrial radio gig ended and he started a daily podcast. Chris Hardwick started **Nerdist**, Marc Maron started **WTF**, and comedy podcasts shot to the top of the charts (joining a plethora of tech-focused podcasts that had been keeping the medium alive).

As iPhone and Android smartphone adoption grew, the podcast mounted its comeback as a viable form of media.

iTunes crossed 1 billion podcast subscriptions in 2013, and hundreds of millions of podcasts are downloaded each month. (It's hard to find an exact number because, in addition to major media corporations, there are tens of thousands of small independent podcasts out there on hundreds—if not thousands—of different topics.)

In 2007, with 261,670 downloads in one month, Ricky Gervais claimed the Guinness World Record for the world's most downloaded podcast. By 2014, This American Life's **Serial** had over 620,000 downloads of each weekly episode!

According to Edison Research's 2016 Infinite Dial study[1], 1 in 5 Americans has listened to a podcast within the last month. That's a 17% jump over 2015, and the largest year-to-year increase in the decade that they've been studying podcasts.

So how does anyone make money off a podcast?

1   Edison Research, *The Infinite Dial 2016* http://www.edisonre-search.com/the-infinite-dial-2016/

A BRIEF HISTORY OF PODCAST ADVERTISING

Podcast advertising might be (relatively) new, but the style of most podcast ads dates back almost 100 years to the early days of radio when stations began selling host-read announcements during their programming. These early sponsorships consisted of "thank you" messages to the companies who made the show possible, and mentions of their products and services.

Over time, audio advertising has evolved to include music, sound effects, and characters, but decades later, the host-read ad can still be heard on the radio—especially endorsement-style ads from popular radio personalities.

Some also compare podcast advertising to the early days of television, when a television show would have a sole sponsor, and the host or characters from the show would perform short commercials or deliver demonstrations during the broadcast. You can occasionally still see this style of advertising, with the host acting as a pitchman, on late-night talk shows.

Modern television advertising has become as diverse as television itself, with many different formats and styles (from cinematic to reality). The more recent trends in television advertising include paid product placement in a show or storyline. This is due in large part to the popularity of the DVR, or services like TiVo. These let users fast forward or skip past advertising.

What's interesting about both radio and television is that their original advertising was "native" to the content: it matched both the format and feel of the show itself but was identified as a paid sponsorship.

In that sense, podcast advertising is a bit of a throwback. While you will occasionally hear ads with elaborate production value, the vast majority of podcast sponsorships consist of host-read ads, personalized with that host's endorsement.

While these personalized ads are less common in the modern radio era, there's a pretty simple reason this format of advertising made the jump to podcasting: many of the early podcasts were hosted by existing or former radio personalities. With them came sponsors and the live-read announcement/thank you.

And since podcasting is a personality-driven medium, podcast ads are most effective when delivered by those same personalities in an engaging and meaningful way.

Of course, the exception to this is the insanely popular *Serial* podcast with its ads for MailChimp—or "MailKimp," as the meme goes. I think this style of advertising is still the exception to the rule, and it's most prevalent on podcasts where the hosts don't want to give an explicit endorsement of a product or service. More on that to follow.

THE STATE OF PODCASTING

Edison Research and Triton Digital publish an annual study called the Infinite Dial, which tracks the media consumption habits of Americans. For a decade now, the Infinite Dial study has been tracking podcasts.

In the 2016 version of this study, they made a few surprising findings:

- 98 million people—more than a one-third of all Americans—have listened to a podcast.

- 57 million—21% of all Americans—have listened to a podcast in the last month. (This is up from 17% in the 2015 study.)

- 20 million—that's 13% of all Americans—have listened to a podcast in the last week. (This represents a 30% increase from 2015.) This last group consumes an average of five podcasts per week.

In 2001, the Infinite Dial study found that the average time spent per day on TV, radio, newspapers, and the internet was 7 hours and 22 minutes. In 2016, it reached 8 hours and 46 minutes. Part of that growth is attributed to podcasts.

They also found that 84% of Americans, ages 25 to 54, own a smartphone. Meanwhile, nearly a third of 18 to 34-year-olds no longer have a radio receiver in their home.

The way we consume media continues to evolve. Can your advertising afford not to evolve with it?

THE STATE OF PODCAST ADVERTISING

At the start of 2016, ZenithOptimedia projected that podcast advertising would generate $35 million in revenue. Norm Pattiz, CEO of PodcastOne, projected it would generate $50 million.

By the end of 2016, the revised estimates were all significantly higher: Bridge Ratings estimated that a total of $167 million was spent in 2016, with projected growth to $243 million in 2017.

But still, it's a very small fraction of the billions that advertisers spend on other digital and broadcast media. Meanwhile, podcast audience numbers continue to show significant growth, and the medium gets bigger with each passing month.

And yet there are (relatively) few advertisers competing in this space.

Even at the start of its second decade, podcasting is still very young. However, there are already enough recurrent brands to offer proof that podcast advertising does indeed work.

This presents a huge opportunity for companies looking to advertise their products and services in this medium.

BRAND AMBITIONS

Many podcasters dream of a day when agencies and big-name brands spend millions to run brand awareness advertising campaigns on podcast networks.

A brand awareness ad campaign consists of advertising that raises brand or product/service awareness and strengthens perception. There might be a call to action, but it's the same across all placements. Most major brands that partake in large-scale campaigns use sophisticated follow-up tracking measures, as well as audience research sampling for recall, to determine their effectiveness in spreading brand recognition. They also look at relevant sales that follow and try to analyze the source of any identifiable spikes.

Brand awareness campaigns are a big deal, and they're how the vast majority of ad dollars are spent through other media channels. Most television ads you see are brand or product/service awareness campaigns. The same goes for radio, print media, and even outdoor advertising like billboards.

A single brand awareness campaign can be worth tens or even hundreds of millions in ad spending, but right now, podcasting isn't getting very much of that money.

With a few exceptions, brand awareness campaigns have all but avoided podcasts because of the higher costs and smaller audience size compared to television, radio, and the web. The biggest podcasts have gotten some of these sought-after advertising dollars from major sponsors, like Ford on the TWiT network and *StartUp*, or Burger King on *The Adam Carolla Show*, but they remain rare.

(A savvy marketer can deduce that whatever Ford or Burger King spent on those podcast advertising campaigns, a major added value for these brands was the press and buzz that came after. When a major company ventures into a new medium, that's news— it shows that they're forward-thinking enough to experiment.)

Brand awareness campaigns tend to favor lower CPM rates (CPM means cost per *mille* or thousand people). Highly specific and targeted promotions may spend more to reach their target audiences, but the bigger the brand, the more people they want to get their message in front of to build awareness.

If a CPM is lower, it also allows for greater sustained repetition throughout a campaign. There is some debate about what "effective frequency" means in this modern era, but there's an old-school marketing adage that a consumer has to be exposed to your brand seven times for your message to rise above the noise, for you to build trust, and for the consumer to take action.

Podcast advertising can greatly accelerate that process, to establish trust with the audience and generate excitement to entice them.

As podcasting continues to grow, expect more major brands to catch on.

DIRECT RESPONSE ADVERTISING

If you have ever heard a podcast ad, you almost certainly heard a direct-response advertisement.

In this case, *direct-response* means the ad uses a URL and/or offer code. This way, if a consumer signs up for their product or service, the advertiser can use that to determine which advertising outlet compelled this customer to take action.

Direct-response advertising exists in many forms. If you've ever clipped a coupon or redeemed a postcard that you got in the mail- you've participated in a form of direct-response advertising. That flyer you redeemed for a new set of tires? Yep, it was direct-response advertising.

In television and radio, the strategy of many direct-response advertisers is to purchase relatively inexpensive ad time in local markets across a handful of stations and times. By using unique offer codes and phone numbers, direct-response advertisers can track which are the most effective. This data will inform advertisers how to shift their dollars accordingly for future campaigns and expand their reach.

In recent years, direct-response advertising on television and radio has also become a popular way to drive people to make purchases on the web. This is why you will sometimes see the same ads on different channels pushing separate URLs or offer codes. Are your customers coming from HGTV or The Food Network? Direct-response marketing can answer this for your business.

After the ad airs, the advertiser can *directly* track what prompted the *response*.

Even though there's a certain science to it, direct-response advertising is often looked down on as a lesser form of marketing. Since direct-response ads can generate results with a few airings on a handful of stations, it costs a fraction of a fraction of what a full-scale brand awareness campaign does.

Because of this lower cost to entry, direct-response advertising is often associated with personal injury attorneys and fly-by-night companies who produce infomercials for "As Seen on TV" products. For most people, "advertising" is what they do on *Mad Men*. It's a creative enterprise and an art form unto itself that doesn't just sell a product, it makes you feel something. "Advertising" is what people go to school for to hone their craft. It's respected. To many, "direct-response advertising" is what made Billy Mays and the Sham Wow guy famous. It's usually associated with cheap airtime, cheap production values, and even cheaper quality products.

Thankfully, that's not what podcast advertising is—and if you've ever looked at a podcast advertising rate card, you know that relative to TV and radio, a podcast's premium audience often carries a premium price. (It certainly isn't cheap.)

However, podcast advertising does utilize the best element of direct-response advertising, which is the ability to track and attribute results.

WHY PODCAST ADVERTISING WORKS

If a traditional advertising campaign is like shouting your message into a crowd, the key strength of podcasting advertising is that it's presented more like a conversation. Your message can be delivered directly to each member of the audience, and the podcast's host is often an ambassador (or evangelist) acting on your behalf.

Even though the CPMs are higher, podcast advertising often requires less repetition to build awareness and strengthen the perception of your product or service.

This approach often makes podcast advertising more effective than other media.

And because you can directly attribute what podcasts worked best for you, your podcast advertising budget can be spent more efficiently over time.

The following chapters will delve into the myriad reasons why podcast advertising works.

ENGAGEMENT

Let's start with the obvious: podcasts are a medium that, by design, listeners engage with actively.

Radio and television are largely passive media. How many times have you listened to a radio station or watched something random on television simply because it was on, or because it was the most attractive option at the time you were making your selection?

Podcasts, by contrast, are sought out by their listeners. They are searched for, subscribed to, and either downloaded or streamed on demand. The last part of that sentence is important. Demand, as in *desire*.

You might be able to advertise on someone's favorite radio show, or on a television show that they watch or DVR regularly, but the nature of a podcast requires hands-on engagement to consume it.

No matter the style of your podcast advertising campaign, you benefit from an engaged audience simply by advertising on a podcast.

THE VOICE INSIDE YOUR HEAD

Regardless of a podcast's topic, its host is almost always someone who is an expert on that topic.

People who listen to the podcast hear that host as an expert or authority, and as someone whose authority is not necessarily limited to the topic of the podcast.

That host is someone the audience listens to, and that is who you want delivering your ad.

After all, we have a strong connection to the voices that we hear inside our head.

If you spend even a short amount of time listening to the radio, an audiobook, or a podcast, you begin to make a connection to the voice you're hearing.

In some scenarios, it feels like you're an audience of one. In others, you feel like a student. After you spend hours listening to that same voice on a daily or weekly basis, it feels just like you're listening to a friend.

Podcast advertising is a huge opportunity to have your message delivered through any of these powerful connections that the listener has with the show's hosts.

EXCITEMENT IS CONTAGIOUS

How many times has a friend or colleague excitedly talked about a restaurant they ate at, inspiring you to dine there as well?

How many times have they purchased a new phone or tablet, talked about how incredible it was and shown it off to you, motivating you to buy one?

How many times have you heard about a website, app, or service from either an expert you follow or someone whose opinion you trust, causing you to take action to try it?

We all have people whose opinions we trust when it comes to various topics. When that person can talk excitedly and at length about something in an animated or entertaining way, it doesn't just catch our attention; it makes us want to be part of the club.

EARLY ADOPTERS ARE AN OPPORTUNITY

As of 2016, 1 in 5 Americans has listened to podcasts within the last month.

If your product or service involves technology in any way, shape, or form—and most products in this day and age do—you don't want to focus your efforts on trying to reach those other 4 out of 5 Americans.

You want to target heavily that 1 in 5.

Why? Because they're early adopters.

Early adoption isn't just a purchasing habit anymore; for many consumers, it's a lifestyle. An early adopter doesn't just embrace new things; they actively seek them out. They are constantly looking for the latest and greatest products and services.

Early adopters don't just read the news about what they love; they spend time reading the rumors. Early adopters don't just pre-order things; they sign up for beta tests. Early adopters don't just buy products on launch day; they line up outside before the store even opens.

Early adopters aren't just trendsetters; they're influencers and often brand ambassadors for the products and services they love. Their later-to-adopt peers look to early adopters to find out what they should be on their radar. In the coming months, these are the same purchases that the late-to-adopt crowd will be making.

An early adopter's interests are far from universal, but for every interest you have, the chances are that you are an early adopter in that area, or that you follow the lead of someone who is.

And mind you, it's not just consumer-focused products and services.

There are early adopters in business as well: forward-thinking entrepreneurs, wantrepreneurs, sidetrepreneurs, small business owners, and efficiency-driven employees who embrace how cutting edge products and services can improve both their productivity and their business.

If you can win over the early adopter, their business, feedback, and word of mouth are ultimately going to help you educate and win over the mainstream audience.

Think of an early adopter like a pre-qualified lead: if your advertising in a niche they're interested in, they're always looking to discover something new, and they're frequently looking to buy.

Podcast advertising is how you can combine the power of authority, expertise, personal connection, and excitement to reach a podcast's engaged audience of early adopters.

HOW PODCAST ADVERTISING WORKS

Advertising on a podcast is different from advertising in other media.

Even if you already know what a CPM is, you may not know how podcast audiences are measured, or the difference in ad styles and formats offered.

In the following chapters, we'll cover the nuts and bolts of how podcast advertising works.

AUDIENCE METRICS

Podcast audience size is measured by the number of unique downloads and streams each episode gets.

For clarity:

Unique usually means one download or stream of a single podcast episode from a single IP address.

A download is when a someone downloads the podcast to their computer or mobile device. They may listen to it immediately, or at a later time.

A stream is when a user starts playing the episode through a podcast client, an app, or a website like iTunes, TuneIn, Stitcher, Spotify, or SoundCloud. The episode starts playing immediately, and depending on the speed of the internet connection, some or all of that episode will download and "buffer" while being listened to.

Because internet speeds, bandwidth costs, and signal strength vary, many users prefer to download their podcasts ahead of time and listen to them later. Many podcast apps for mobile devices offer this feature as well—and if you've ever dealt with minutes of driving in silence because you lost your signal, or paid extra cellular data fees on your bill, you know why.

Take the total number of unique downloads and streams for each episode, and you have that episode's audience size.

Almost every podcaster takes their **consistent** number of downloads and streams per episode, and rounds down to set their rates. The idea is that they are guaranteeing a minimum number of downloads and streams per episode that you will be advertising on. (They do not take into account huge spikes from a marquee guest or a promoted episode—when those occur, it's just a bonus for the advertiser on that particular episode.)

Skeptics and naysayers (usually from other ad-supported media) have a pretty common critique of this model: How do you know that the person who downloads the episode **actually** listens to it? How do you know that someone who starts listening to the episode makes it all the way to hear the ads?

Of course, you don't know either with 100% certainty, but consider this:

Whatever that consistent number of downloads and streams is represents an engaged audience who makes a regular effort to download and stream the podcast.

Let's compare that to limitations measuring audience size in more traditional media:

• Television

Ratings are determined based on a (relatively) small sampling of individuals and their television-viewing habits. The ratings and demographic sampling often determine the price for advertising on each television show for an individual airing. Methodology aside, DVRs make it incredibly easy to skip past ads, sites like Hulu sell commercial space on streaming versions of the show, and Netflix eliminates the ads altogether. Even if someone watches the episode live when broadcast, who is to say that they don't leave the room to fix a snack or use the restroom during the ad break?

- Radio

Ratings are determined based on a (relatively) small sampling of individuals and their radio-listening habits. In some cases, radio reporting services are not tracking individual radio shows being listened to, but are instead reporting on the times of day and time spent listening to individual radio stations. This data is used to make estimations about that radio station's larger audience and reach, and that number is used to set the advertising rates. I don't know about you, but given the length and randomness of most radio advertising I hear, I feel an ad break is a great opportunity to switch to another station.

- Print Media

Ad rates aren't just based on the number of copies printed per issue. Stacks of unread magazines aside, did you know that circulation numbers often include an additional increase in numbers to reflect the assumption that each issue of the publication will be passed on to one or more people?

- Banner advertising

Do you run an ad blocker? According to PageFair, ad blocking users grew to 45 million people in 2015, and that's in the United States alone. If your target audience is remotely tech savvy, banner advertising is likely not to reach them. (And when content requires a viewer to disable their ad blocker to view it, many will instead stop visiting that site.)

These examples aren't meant to attack other forms of advertising, but instead to acknowledge that every form of advertising has its weaknesses and areas of concern when it comes to metrics. None of this has stopped any of the above from being multi-billion-dollar industries that are highly effective for advertisers.

Furthermore, most podcasts and networks set their advertising rates at the beginning of each year or quarter, based on the consistent number of downloads per episode in the previous year or quarter.

With the way podcast consumption is growing by double-digit percentages from year to year, most podcasts are consistently over delivering on their guaranteed numbers, which represents another nice value add for their advertisers.

CPMs

CPM stands for Cost Per Mille (thousand in Latin).

Multiply the CPM by the number of thousands of the consistent audience size for a single episode, and you have the per-episode cost to advertise on a podcast.

Typically, this cost is per ad unit. Some podcasts sell different ad opportunities on the same episode of the podcast at different CPM rates. Others will require you to buy multiple units in the same episode, and many bundle the ad units together and offer incentive pricing to purchase them.

Many podcasts offer CPMs in the $10 to $50 range, but those with premium audiences come at a premium price, and it's not uncommon to see $60 or even $100 CPMs on podcasts that cater to a highly desirable, heavily engaged audience.

Yes. These prices are higher than other media.

I've seen many an advertiser freak-out over or take issue with the relatively high cost of podcast advertising.

Not the total cost of the campaign, nor the cost to purchase individual episodes, but rather the cost to reach a single member of that podcast's audience.

To that skepticism, I offer the next chapter.

ALL CPMs ARE NOT CREATED EQUAL

Podcast advertising isn't about getting your message in front of the most people; it's about getting your message in front of the *right* people.

Yes, you can purchase advertising in other media for as low as a few dollars per thousand reached. But what percentage of that audience is the right fit for your product or service? Of that small percentage (or fraction thereof), how many are going to pay attention to your advertising amidst the noise and the clutter of every other advertiser looking for low-cost customer acquisition?

Podcast advertising offers you a huge opportunity to reach a highly engaged, targeted audience with advertising that communicates your message in an authentic and passionate way. No clutter, no noise—just your message presented in the context of the show's content.

Think of a podcast audience as representing qualified leads. Based on the podcast subject matter or demographics, the majority of this audience is your *target audience*.

Yes, you might be spending more to reach each potential customer, but you're reaching people with a much higher likelihood of becoming your customers.

Combine this with the authoritative delivery to that audience, and it's easy to understand why podcast advertising offers an opportunity that's much greater than those other, cheaper means of advertising.

PODCAST ADVERTISING PLACEMENT POSITIONS

If you know anything about podcast advertising, you probably know what the pre-roll, the interstitial or mid-roll, and the post-roll ads are.

Pre-Roll ad:
An ad that occurs near the beginning of the episode.

Interstitial or Mid-Roll ad:
An ad that occurs as a break from the content of the episode.

Post-Roll ad:
An ad that occurs at the end of the episode.

Actual lengths and formats vary per podcaster, but in general, pre- and post-rolls tend to be 15 to 30 seconds, whereas mid-rolls can be anywhere from 30 seconds to 3 minutes in length.

There's debate and varying preference over the effectiveness of the pre-roll and post-roll ad placements on their own, but the consensus is that interstitial or mid-roll advertising is the most desirable.

My personal experience is that having multiple placements within the same episode works best. Many networks require either a combination of pre-roll and mid-roll ads, and I think that's smart for two reasons:

First, it gives the audience an initial exposure to your brand's support of the show, followed by lengthier messaging that reinforces who you are, what you're offering, and your call to action.

Second, it keeps podcasters from selling each ad position separately, creating a scenario where you have too many advertisers   placing ads on a single episode for any single advertiser's message to be effective.

One thing to consider: the post-roll ad is frequently dismissed with the assumption that since it's at the end of the episode, it gets tuned out or skipped over.

I disagree. The post-roll is an undervalued add-on, and I think it presents an excellent opportunity for an additional connection with the audience.

When combined with placements earlier in the episode, a post-roll ad is a great complement to an earlier ad, as it's an opportunity to have the host remind the audience to answer your call to action once they finish the episode.

PODCAST ADVERTISING STYLES

Short-format podcast ads, like pre-rolls, are usually recorded separately from the content of the episode itself. They can be pre-produced, but when paired with a later ad placement, they are usually read by the podcast host.

Interstitial or mid-roll ads usually follow one of three different presentation styles:

1. The sponsor-produced ad
    This is similar to a radio spot, and it can use music, sound effects, a voiceover artist, or a spokesperson for your company. It often ends with a clear call to action.

2. The host-read produced ad
    Delivered by the host of the show it will be appearing on. It may contain production elements. It often contains sponsor messaging and sometimes an interview with a sponsor's representative or customer. It ends with a clear call to action.

3. The host-read integrated ad
    This ad is read by the host of the show and is usually (but not always*) delivered within the context of the episode. It contains only live production elements, and within the flow of the show, it has the same feel as the show's content. It ends with a clear call to action to support the sponsor's brand building or direct response objectives.

*This live-style ad read can be recorded separately and inserted into the show before publishing, but given the host's delivery and style of the ad, it is important that it match the rest of the episode's production, recording quality, and sound levels.

The third style, the interstitial or mid-roll **integrated** ad is my favorite. Why? Because even though it's labeled an advertisement, it feels native to the show itself and flows within the context and the content of the episode.

When the ad is a part of the show, sometimes the podcast's co-hosts or guests will chime in and contribute their personal experience or ask questions about a sponsor's product or service.

When this happens, you've created not only an endorsement but also a discussion around your talking points that ends with your call to action. It starts with a clear distinction that it's an ad or sponsored placement, but to the listener, it feels like content.

By comparison, an advertiser-produced ad can be an abrupt change. It interrupts the listening experience and is more likely to be skipped or tuned out by fans of the show. It also separates your message from the context of the episode. A host-read, pre-recorded ad maintains the tone and voice of the podcast content, and I do think it is an effective and viable second choice for hosts that do not record their ads within their episodic content.

However, some podcast hosts record one incredible version of their personal endorsement and re-use that same ad over and over. My recommendation to advertisers (and podcasters) is that the host records a few different versions of the ad to rotate between, so the listener is less inclined to tune out due to repetition.

WILL PODCAST ADVERTISING WORK FOR YOU?

The big question: What can podcast advertising do for your business or brand?

In the following chapters, I'll cover the key factors that can help you determine if podcast advertising is a good fit to advertise your product or service.

WHAT ARE YOU ADVERTISING?

Awareness campaigns aside, you may have noticed a theme with the types of products and services that advertise on podcasts:

They either want to give you a free trial to their service (hoping that you like it and convert into a paying subscriber), or they want to sell you a stand-alone product that usually costs $20 or more.

With a subscription offer, you make your money over the course of months or years. Whether you're selling software as a service, a monthly box of goodies, or anything with a monthly fee attached, each customer's lifetime value can range from hundreds to thousands of dollars. The better your service and the more value you provide, the longer your customers subscribe, and the more money that customer is worth to you.

(In addition to driving sign-ups for new subscriptions with your podcast ads, you're also advertising to many of your current subscribers and reminding them of your value so they won't cancel their subscriptions. This is why the same subscription services have sponsored many of the same podcasts for almost a decade.)

With a one-time purchase, on the other hand, you recoup your advertising expenses through profit margin, some form of an upsell, an add-on service, or repeat business.

Even if your company is new, you have an idea of what that average customer lifetime value target is, or what your profit margin will be, which gives you a sense of how much each customer-acquisition is worth to you (to compare against podcast advertising costs).

Every advertiser has a formula for what percentage of listeners they would need to convert into customers to make a podcast advertising campaign successful. Often, they will compare that against lower conversion percentages they've experienced with advertising in other mediums. This is a mistake.

Depending on how a podcast's subject matter and demographics align with your target audience--and if executed properly--podcast advertising can perform better for you than *most* media, and you can turn any risk you take with podcasts into a well-calculated one.

But first...

THE REASONS WHY SOME PODCAST ADVERTISING CAMPAIGNS FAIL

There are several scenarios in which podcast advertising may not be as effective for you:

- Your business model or pricing is untested or unproven.

If your product or service is new and you're still testing it, that's fine. Podcast advertising can be a wonderful tool for working with early adopters to solicit feedback. But if you're unsure of what to charge, go with charging less to incentivize your first customers to sign up now and lock in that price. If and when you settle on a higher price, your first customers will be less likely ever to cancel and lose their sweetheart subscription rate.

- You make your profit off hidden shipping charges or add-ons.

"Wow, those flowers sure sounded cheap until I got to the last page of the checkout process and saw that the shipping cost was twice as expensive as the bouquet of flowers."

"What's this $17.95 handling charge for, exactly?"

- You have bad reviews to the point that "rip-off" is a prominent phrase in your Google search results.

Regardless of the ad and the endorsement, podcast fans are smart and will usually read up on a new product or service if they've never heard of it before. If you don't have good reviews to back up your ad, smart customers won't be buying. They also won't be as trusting with that podcast's sponsors in the future.

- You require an email address just to browse your site, or to learn more about your product or service.

No one likes being greeted with a pop-up the first time they visit a website. Don't make customers give you their email address before they enter the checkout process.

- You run better offers, discounts, or lower prices through other channels.

If a simple Google search for a promo code turns up a better offer than what I heard on the podcast, can you guess which code I'll use? (Take *that*, podcast offer code!)

- Your company name or URL has a unique spelling that no one can figure out from hearing it.

If your company or domain has a funky spelling, the name had better be short enough that it can be spelled out in less than seven letters. It may look cool written, but this is a spoken-word medium.

- Your limited-time offer is extremely limiting, expiring too soon.

"I went back and listened to an interview from last month with an author I liked. I tried to use the offer code when I signed up, but it gave me an error and said it was expired already."

THE AUDIENCE MUST ALWAYS WIN

There's one big disclaimer to all of this, and believe it or not, I've met both podcasters and advertisers who cannot seem to wrap their heads around it:

In my experience, endorsement-style advertising works best when the host is genuinely excited about the product or service AND the advertiser delivers a positive customer experience for the audience.

The risk that it won't is why some hosts don't add their personal endorsement or experience to their ads. They'll take the advertiser's money and they'll read the ad, but they'll stop short of personally endorsing it. This is because they want an "out" if things go sidewise and the association could potentially damage their credibility.

(Of course, an endorsement is still inferred by the advertiser's association with the podcast and its hosts.)

There are also some hosts/networks out there that will advertise and endorse any product or service that wants to sponsor their podcast. (I'm not telling tales out of school here. Some podcast hosts have bragged about this in interviews and during their podcasts.)

In both of these cases, if the audience feels disgruntled by their experience with the advertiser they are liable to complain to the network and hosts. In the eyes of the affected fans, it can seriously damage the credibility of both that podcast and its host.

The trust a podcast audience has in the podcast host is incredibly important. It's why this medium works.

When working with a new advertiser, I heavily research and screen any potential clients to make sure the reviews are good and that they deliver. (If it's a company I'm not familiar with, I'll even do a stealth sign up to get a first-hand customer experience.) I also make it clear to sponsors that they're going to have to do right by any audience I help deliver to them.

If you can't do right by the audience, you probably shouldn't be advertising on podcasts.

For podcasters, authenticity and excitement are key to delivering a message. If it's a product or service that you can use personally, you need to use it and love it (and not just because you might get paid to).

If it's something outside of what you have a personal use for, you need to be able to understand it and how it's benefiting others. Either way, you need to be a true believer and excited to share it with your audience.

If you can't do that for an advertiser, you probably shouldn't be advertising them on your podcast.

The business of podcast advertising is about creating win-win-win situations: the advertiser wins, the podcaster wins, and—most importantly and always—the audience wins.

YOUR FIRST PODCAST ADVERTISING CAMPAIGN

Now that you know why podcast advertising works, how it works, and how it can work for you, it's time to explore how to go about conducting your first podcast advertising campaign.

In the following chapters, we'll cover the steps and key things to consider, as well as the best practices for running your campaign and helpful advice.

AGENCIES, BROKERS, AND DIY

As it currently stands, you can reach out to someone at most podcasts or networks to discuss advertising with them. Depending on the size and how established the podcast is, either the host or a producer, agent, or broker already working with them can answer your questions and offer you information and options to sponsor their shows.

Alternatively, many podcasts are part of a network. These networks have an in-house sales arm or a designated network broker for their sales and ads.

Lastly, there are agencies. Agencies help you find, research, and manage relationships with one or more podcasts, networks, or brokers.

Having worked in all of the above capacities in selling and placing ads on podcasts, I prefer working as an agent. Not only does it give advertisers a knowledgeable ally and advocate in the process, but it also often costs them the same as (or less than) going direct.

An agency like my own, ADOPTER Media, typically gets paid a commission by the podcasters because we are making their jobs easier and bringing them business. Our clients get the value of our expertise and services, the podcasters get value from having to do less work so they can focus their podcasts, and everybody wins.

SELECTING PODCASTS

When selecting which podcasts to advertise on, I recommend looking to the following criteria:

- Subject Matter
  If the podcast's main subject matter is any way related to the product or service you will be advertising, it's a natural fit.

- Audience Demographics
  This is not as obvious, and it's where an agency such as ours can be of help. Most serious podcasters and networks conduct audience research of some sort. They know their audience demographics as they relate to income, job title, function, spending habits, and interests. If you know a bit about your target audience, you can see if it matches up with who the podcasts are reaching.

- The Host
  This takes a bit of research, but let's say you're offering a coffee-related product, and the host of a popular car-related podcast is a huge coffee aficionado who goes off on coffee-related tangents on his podcast. In addition to the podcast's primary topic, the show's audience also trusts the host's opinion on coffee (or any other secondary topics that they're passionate about and bring up from time to time). While not the most obvious advertising opportunity, it's one I've seen used to great effect by savvy sponsors who

do their research (or work with someone like myself who does).

- Follow the Lead of Others
  If a comparable product or service—or one whose audience you have found is similar to yours—is repeatedly advertising on a podcast, follow their lead.

In the next two chapters, I'll expand more on that last point to give you insight into how you make your podcast selection process even more effective.

FOLLOW A LEADER

I once read that a certain popular sandwich chain doesn't do any traditional market research when choosing locations for their new restaurants. Instead, they look for where a popular coffee chain has opened multiple stores in the same neighborhood, and the sandwich chain opens a restaurant there.

Their reasoning is that the two businesses' audience overlap is high. If a location is working well for the coffee chain, chances are good it will also work well for the sandwich chain.

If you're reading this book, you may have been given the ~~assignment~~ opportunity to research if podcast advertising is the right fit for your company or client.

Some potential advertisers I've spoken to request case studies or white papers that outline specific situations and actions from brands, outlining their spending, their return on investment, and every step they took to get there.

Most advertisers never share specifics about campaign performance with podcasters, let alone grant permission to share that data with other potential advertisers. Why? It's sensitive information about their business that they don't want to share. There are some case studies out there provided by networks and agencies, but of course, they're all success stories. I suggest taking them with a grain of salt and considering if they are relevant to your company.

Here's what I recommend instead:

1. Listen to a handful of episodes of the podcast you are considering. Who are the sponsors? (Some podcasts make it even easier to identify their advertisers by listing them on their sponsor page or the individual episode's show notes.)

2. Take note of individual sponsors.

3. Is there a sponsor with product or service offerings similar to yours in any way (not necessarily a competitor)? Is there an advertiser with similar demographic targets?

4. Do those sponsors appear on multiple episodes of that podcast? Have they been a regular sponsor if you listen back to episodes from months or years ago?

If you do this enough, you will start to notice certain patterns. You can track long-term successes as well as gain insight from short-term campaigns that didn't repeat.

But if there's a clear coffee shop to your sandwich chain, you may want to target that same neighborhood and open up shop.

REPEAT BUSINESS SPEAKS VOLUMES

If a podcast is established and sustains repeat business from many of the same advertisers, you can conclude that the audience numbers and CPM rates are acceptable metrics to the market in determining its pricing.

I've yet to work with a single company that didn't primarily look at their return on investment (ROI) to determine the success of a campaign. For different companies, ROI can mean different things. For a product, it's profit vs. spend. For a service, it's the number of signups they get multiplied by the projected customer lifetime value vs. what they spent on ad placement. For a branding campaign, it can be sales, website traffic, social media activity, or a variety of other indicators.

I've found the following questions to be the most consistent means of determining whether an advertiser is doing well on a particular podcast: has that advertiser been on multiple episodes within the same month? Have they repeatedly advertised over a quarter? Have they been sponsoring the show for six months or longer?

More than any other metric, an advertiser's repeat business demonstrates sustained ROI .

Regardless of your company or target audience, I know that if you keep coming back and buying more advertising on a specific podcast, it's performing for you.

MINIMIZING RISK WITH NEW CAMPAIGNS

I get it. You want to test podcast advertising or a new network with minimal risk.

Based on earlier chapters, you've seen how you can turn that into a calculated risk.

Every podcast and network has a minimum buy-in amount. For some, it can be a few episodes, for others, it can be in the thousands (or tens of thousands) of dollars.

There are a few reasons for this:

First, it can take *some* repetition for podcast advertising to demonstrate its effectiveness—not seven times, like the old adage would have you believe, but it often takes more than hearing one ad. Yes, some products and services generate revenue after the first ad placement, but most take a few placements to gain traction.

Second, the time it takes to screen, educate, and onboard a new advertiser isn't worth it for a single-episode commitment. It's just not—unless you're talking about a podcast with an incredibly large audience.

But the third reason, and perhaps the most important one, is that a podcaster's connection with their community has great value. It's the most important asset that a podcaster has.

Every time they do an ad, they are tapping into the credibility and trust that they have built with their audience. If they have too many new and different advertisers with every episode—each advertising just once as a test—it would spread the host's credibility too thin and diminish the advertising value to where everyone's ads would be less special, and, therefore, less effective.

Additionally, a minimum buy-in requirement levels the playing field for advertisers. It shows that you're making a commitment toward building a relationship, and as a result, you will get the same level of care and attention as their other established advertisers.

You might be able to negotiate with some podcasters on their minimum. However, if a podcast already has a lot of advertisers or sells out far in advance, the minimum buy-in requirement isn't open for negotiation.

CAMPAIGN SCHEDULING AND REPETITION

Ad frequency is a common question, especially when faced with your first podcast advertising campaign.

Strategies vary based on the product or service, but here's what I've found to be true:

The more you are *asking* from the audience, the more you need to *invest* in repeat ads to see results.

Let's say you're selling a $20 per month, consumer-focused subscription service with a free trial. A handful of ads on any podcast should prove whether or not this medium is a good fit for you, and you'll likely start seeing results after the first few episodes you sponsor.

(I've found the same to be true when selling $100 one-time-purchase products. To affluent early adopters, that's an impulse buy.)

On the other hand, even if you're selling a $20/month, business-targeted service, you might need a half dozen placements on a podcast before you can properly gauge its impact on your bottom line. Why? Because most people are more cautious when making business-related decisions, and it's important that they hear a few ads highlighting different aspects of your product or service and build familiarity with your brand.

In the latter scenario, you're not asking them to trust you as a consumer, but as a business. Whether they're entrepreneurs, decision makers, or decision influencers at a company, business credibility matters.

If you're offering a business-targeted product or service, a high-priced consumer product, or anything that requires a consumer to make a big decision regarding their time or money, you should plan for greater repetition in a shorter amount of time, or placements spread out over a longer period to really see results.

If you have a consumer-targeted, relatively low-cost product or service, a shorter-term campaign (think 3- to 6-weeks) is often an effective test.

Notice I said weeks and not episodes. Here's why: you don't need to advertise on every episode of a podcast. In my experience, every other episode is often just as effective. (For a show that releases daily episodes, 5 to 7 days a week, you can also do every day for a week and then alternate taking a week off.)

If you're on a network with its own fan base, alternating between weeks on different shows is also effective. Why? Because most podcast networks have fans who consume multiple shows on the network, and there's some overlap between different audiences for individual podcasts on the same network. In this scenario, some of the audience hears about you in multiple places, further reinforcing your messaging and building trust.

OFFER CODES AND URLS

If you've ever heard a podcast ad, then you've almost definitely heard a podcast offer (and its attached offer code or special landing page URL).

The idea is simple: you're giving the audience an incentive to act upon hearing your ad and, perhaps just as important, let you know exactly where they heard it.

This code is sometimes called an offer code, coupon code, discount code, or promo code. It's almost always a code that you enter in the shopping cart during the checkout process. (This works well if you want to drive traffic to your main URL, and then let users enter the code after going through your existing landing page.)

Some advertisers also prefer to use a special landing page URL that follows the format of sponsordomain.com/podcastname or sponsordomain.com/networkname. This drives traffic to a customized landing page or a special entry point to your website as part of your campaign.

Maybe you want to highlight a particular product or aspect of your service for the podcast audience? That's just one way you can use a customized landing page to your advantage.

I normally recommend using a custom landing page URL and an offer code together. Sometimes a landing page automatically applies the offer code or discount at checkout, but I think it's good to have both because visitors might go to your main website and use the code.

Remember: using an offer code is the single easiest way to give direct attribution to sales and sign-ups generated by your podcast advertising campaign. Make the offer good enough that people will remember the special URL or offer code and use it.

While I'm on the subject of best practices:

Make sure that your offer codes and URLs match the name of the network or podcast you're advertising on and are consistent from episode to episode!

It's fine to want to track which networks and individual podcasts are producing the best results, but don't try to get extra-granular and track results by each episode of that podcast you sponsor.

Think of it this way: you want the audience to remember your product/service, why they want to try it, and a URL or offer code.

If they are going to hear your ad multiple times, why are you trying to confuse them with multiple, unique offer codes?

Keep it simple!

WHAT'S THE OFFER?

So you've got your offer code, but what should your offer be?

If you're offering a service or a subscription, a free trial is a must. Combined with a discounted subscription rate, it's even better.

If you're offering a product, you should be offering a discount of 10%—or, at the very least, free shipping. You want to incentivize the audience to act, and also to use the offer code.

But while your special offer should be enticing, it shouldn't be a lesser value than promotions you're running through other channels.

Your podcast advertising offer-based incentive needs to match your other existing offers outside of podcasts. If you have any coupon out in the wild that offers a greater incentive to use it than your podcast offers, the podcast audience is savvy, and enough of them will find it via Google to where it will obfuscate or detract from the effectiveness of your podcast advertising campaign. (It also hurts a podcaster's credibility with their community, which can tarnish your relationship with the podcaster.)

CREATING PODCAST ADS THAT WORK

If you refer to the story of the first podcast advertising that I ever heard, the ManGrate ad on Adam Carolla's podcast, you can gain insight into how to craft an effective mid-roll podcast ad delivered by the show's host.

Pre-roll and post-roll ads are short and usually tightly scripted by the advertiser. You want to state the advertiser's name, their slogan (or what they do), and a call to action with an incentive-based offer code or URL. These are mostly short, sweet, and to the point—a pre-roll or "top of show" ad usually sets up your later ad placement, and a post-roll is a reminder of the ad they heard earlier.

It's during the host read, mid-roll ad that you have a real opportunity to make a connection.

You want to tell a story or, at the very least, present a hook that captures the listener's attention. This can be done by either presenting a common problem, contextualizing your product or service within recent news, or—better yet—having the host share something that they love with their audience.

That's why host enthusiasm is so important.

In the case of a consumer-facing product or service, it's mandatory that the host has used it and was a fan.

With a B2B-facing product or service, make sure that the host understands it and has contextual relevance for its strengths.

From there, it's simply a matter of providing the host with key talking points to touch upon, and ending with a clear call to action that drives them to your website to learn more and purchase or subscribe.

Interstitial talking points should always be less than one page. It sounds simple, but I've seen many advertisers try to overcomplicate it or cram in too much information. A good rule is that if your talking points are too long, create multiple versions and rotate them throughout the campaign.

Additionally, make sure the hosts have access to your product or service well in advance of the campaign. Give them a one-sheet or a rough draft of your advertising talking points, but consider that a starting point.

It's very important that hosts fully understand your product or service—and your messaging—before the campaign starts. If they have questions, chances are their audience will as well. This can help guide how to market to their audience.

Whenever possible, incorporate in the host's suggestions. Also, make sure to touch upon the reasons why the host is passionate about your product and service on the final talking points and ad copy.

This extra bit of preparation can make a huge difference in your podcast ads.

A LOOK TO THE FUTURE

Podcast advertising is evolving. This year saw the expansion of dynamic advertising, which allows different ads served to different listeners.

Currently, there are two ways this is implemented.

The first is a refresh method that essentially lets you rent ad space on all episodes of a podcast for a day, a week, or a month. I don't mean just the podcasts released during those times, but rather your ads get placed on every single episode of the podcast that is downloaded or streamed during the duration of your ad campaign (including older episodes).

These podcasts feature ads read by the show hosts, the ads just change from week to week or month to month. Very few podcasts and networks are doing this at the moment.

The second method is even more advanced and limited to only a few innovators in the industry, and that is dynamically inserting ads based on your geography, or your demographic data if you're on their website or app.

I can see why this is appealing, especially for shows with wide appeal that don't lend themselves to a particular demographic based on subject matter.

However, I think it will become challenging to maintain podcast advertising's uniquely personal touch if the latter form ever gains wide acceptance.

Many new podcast networks have also recently launched, some which represent the entertainment industry and mainstream media taking notice. It will be interesting to see if these shows are able to establish the same level of personal connection that many audiences feel with independent podcasters.

IN CONCLUSION

Writing this book has been a distillation of years' worth of oft-repeated observations and conversations into written form, and reflecting on the most frequent and common advice that applies to *most* advertisers and podcasters I've worked with.

(Of course, as with all things your mileage may vary, but if you have a uniquely new or different situation, I am up for the challenge.)

In this process, I also started taking stock of the impact that podcasts and podcast advertising have had on my life and purchasing decisions: For instance, we launched the ADOPTER Media website on Squarespace, I sleep on a Casper Mattress, and I listen to most of my books via Audible. Not only that, but I learned how to publish this book through lynda.com, and if you signed up for my mailing list, you did it through MailChimp.

Why did I choose these services? Personal endorsement ads from passionate podcast hosts.

This might sound crazy, but because of the time I've spent listening to podcasts, I now feel like I know a few podcasts hosts better than some of my friends and family members. When a podcast host that I respect or admire is passionate about a product or service, it piques my interest.

As podcasting is now well into its second decade, we can see that the fundamentals haven't changed since its introduction, but as a medium, it continues to mature and welcome new listeners, podcasters, and advertisers into the fold on a daily basis.

It's an exciting time.

Thank you for taking the time to read this book. I hope it has helped you understand more about podcasting and podcast advertising.

I welcome your questions, feedback, etc. My email address is glenn@adopter.media, and I am happy to help anyone looking to establish or grow their podcast advertising plans.

Of course, as podcasting and podcast advertising evolves, this guide will continue to as well.

Be sure to visit http://adopter.media/list to be notified of future editions of this book, and follow our podcast advertising blog for regular updates.

ABOUT THE AUTHOR

Glenn Rubenstein is the founder of ADOPTER Media. He has previously worked at TWiT and editorial outlets like CNet and Gamespot. He has also written for publications such as Wired Magazine and the San Francisco Examiner.

He lives in Northern California, and to this day, he still considers ordering a ManGrate grill accessory to give his tofu that "steakhouse" taste.

FREE EBOOK & EXECUTIVE SUMMARY

Thanks again for reading this book and delving into the world of podcast advertising. I hope you enjoyed it and learned a thing or two.

As my way of saying "thank you" for reading the first edition of my book, I'd like to give you the Executive Summary and the eBook version for FREE.

Please visit http://adopter.media/bookbonus to take advantage of this offer.

JOIN THE
MAILING LIST

Want to be notified about new publications and important podcast advertising news?

Join the ADOPTER Media mailing list!

Sign up at: http://adopter.media/list

HAVE QUESTIONS OR FEEDBACK?

Email hello@adopter.media and we'll respond directly.

Also, we're already working on the 2017 edition and value your feedback.

Let us know if there are any additional aspects of podcast advertising that you'd like to see covered in the next edition of this book.